Beach Boundaries

Fences and Gates of the Los Angeles Area Beach Cities

Linda Byrne
Robert Scott

Schiffer Publishing Ltd
4880 Lower Valley Road • Atglen, PA • 19310

Library of Congress Control Number: 2011946215

Designed by Danielle D. Farmer
Cover Design by Bruce M. Waters
Type set in Brisa/Browalia New

ISBN: 978-0-7643-4097-0
Printed in China

Published by Schiffer Publishing Ltd.
4880 Lower Valley Road, Atglen, PA 19310
Phone: (610) 593-1777
Fax: (610) 593-2002
E-mail: Info@schifferbooks.com

Dedication

We dedicate this book to
DONN BYRNE & FOSTER SCOTT,
who are inspirational gardeners
and terrific fathers.

Acknowledgments

We are most grateful to Gayle Noguchi who helped edit thousands of photos. Jan Dennis, of Manhattan Beach, and Jolie Carpenter, of Signature Publishing Group, provided ideas and encouragement to get this project started. And thank you to Jeri Dearden of the Manhattan Beach Cultural Heritage Conservancy for her support.

In Europe, Schiffer books are distributed by
Bushwood Books, 6 Marksbury Ave., Kew Gardens
Surrey TW9 4JF England
Phone: 44 (0) 20 8392 8585
Fax: 44 (0) 20 8392 9876
E-mail: info@bushwoodbooks.co.uk
Website: www.bushwoodbooks.co.uk

Contents

Introduction

Small fences and gates abound at the beach.

Visitors to the beach communities may be intrigued to find so many residential properties defined by decorative fences and gates. Here, fences are not necessarily used to confine the dog or keep out unwanted visitors, but instead, can simply exist as a visual marker of personal space.

Neighbors share a continuous picket fence.

Defining personal space.

Demarcating property lines.

255

The high cost of real estate along the Pacific Coast dictates an increased density of living. The closer to the beach one lives, the smaller the residential lots become, and square footage for living sells at a premium. Front and back lawns are tiny, if they exist at all. As the lot size decreases, the number of houses surrounded by fences increases. Fences are used to mark off and enclose these small spaces. Often the fences surrounding these lawns are diminutive, too. They serve to soften the harshness of the concrete streets and walks, and to mitigate the proximity of the next home. The charm of a little fence also helps negate the scale of the mega houses that are frequently squeezed onto tiny lots that vie for views and closeness to the ocean. The small boundaries help divide neighbors but still connect homes to the beach vibe.

Balancing scale.

Connecting to the beach vibe.

A classic beach property.

Fences as Boun

aries

A quaint fence serving a purpose.

Curb appeal is defined as the first thing visitors see as they approach a home. The curb appeal of a picket fence is obvious, but some boundaries go beyond aesthetics. The fences here are almost necessary and have evolved as a compromise between the need for privacy and the desire to live in a compact seaside community. With space tight, small fences are functional while not visually reducing the home's yard.

This fence is not meant to fence out the world.

Curb appeal.

Creating privacy.

Fences can screen off beach gear, unattractive views, or service areas.

A fence can be a physical or visual barrier.

Compact living.

Fences are almost necessary for homes located on the Walk Streets.

Front lawns become porches.

The term ***Walk Streets*** is a part of the beach vernacular to denote areas closest to the ocean where home entrances face a common pedestrian sidewalk, which leads to the beach. Streets and driveways that serve these homes are in alleys at the rear of the house. The front lawns off these pedestrian walks are miniscule at best and lawns become the "front porch" or threshold to family life. It is common for these lawns to be delineated by small fences.

Outdoor Walls

Additional living space.

One of the beauties of Southern California living is that outdoor spaces can be used year around. Since there is little need to protect from the elements here, the front lawns of many homes extend the living space and serve as outdoor rooms. Outdoor rooms help smaller dwellings feel significantly bigger and connect homeowners to their environment. Fences become the outdoor walls and can give a pleasant sense of privacy while providing seclusion for outdoor family entertaining and relaxing.

Outdoor spaces opening to Walk Streets.

Indoor spaces open to outdoor spaces.

An open design lets in light while providing privacy.

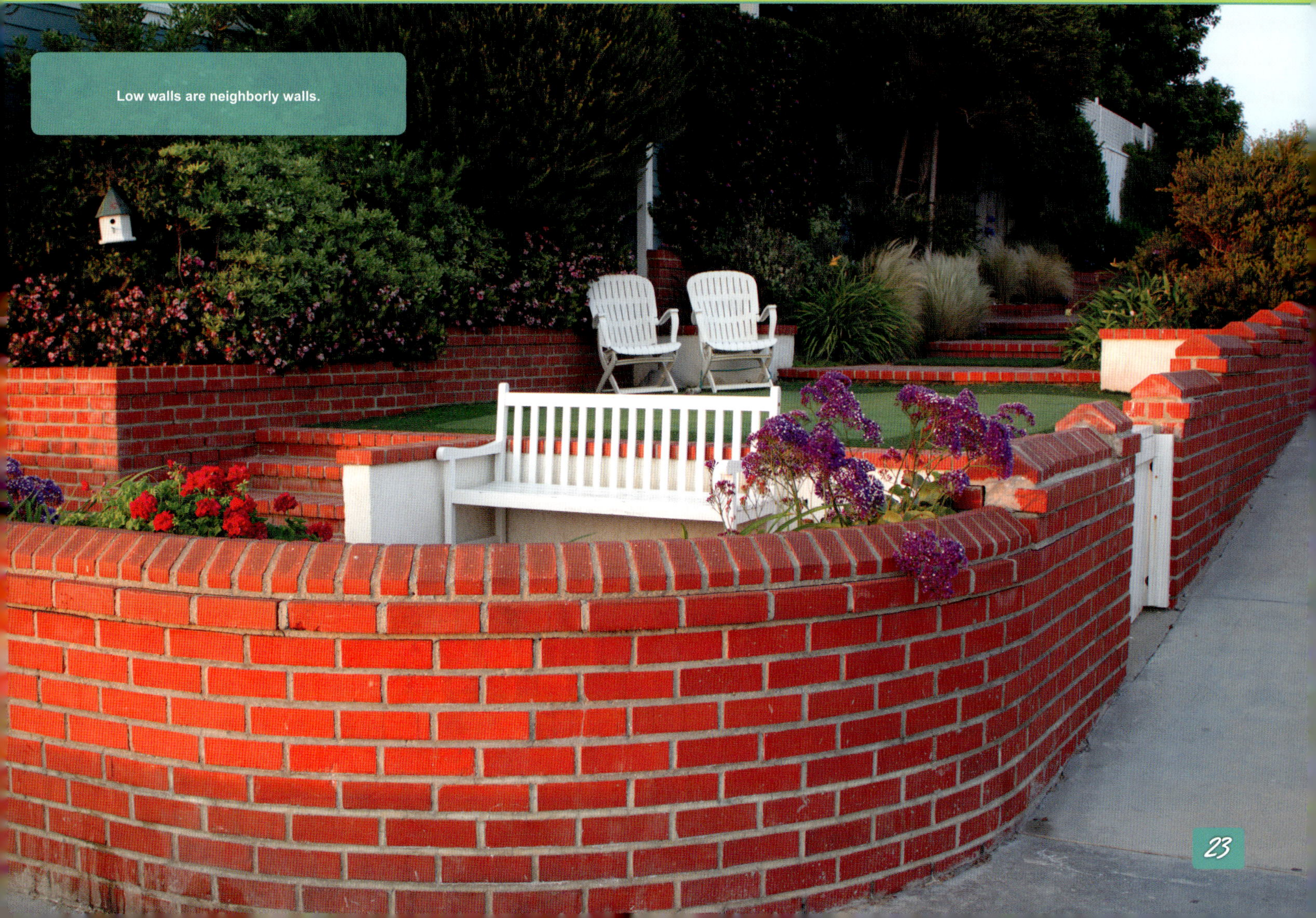

Low walls are neighborly walls.

1215
Seventeenth

A wall with a welcoming entry.

Fence or wall?

Styles and Ma

erials

Painted steel and railroad ties.

Homebuilders and designers have incorporated small stucco walls and other building materials, landscaping, or ornamentation, as well as the traditional picket fence to divide public and private spaces. The best fences are integrated or complimentary to the design or style of the house. Fence construction utilizes all kinds of materials. Can stainless steel, even concrete block, ever be considered charming? Some of these boundaries push the boundary of typical fencing material but fences can be elegant and sophisticated even amongst the casual beach life style.

Elegant in its simplicity, split rail.

Steel cable.

Vertical steel rods.

Rusted steel panels and painted posts.

Industrial materials, yet beautiful.

Ivy trimmed to a lattice design on a stucco wall.

Painted to match the home.

Modern detailing on a stucco wall.

Casual and simple, yet effective design.

Craftsman styling.

Brick pavers contribute to the charm.

Lattice design atop painted concrete block.

Glass panels enclose a raised deck.

A mid-century fence, still fashionable.

A classic horizontal design.

A more modern approach with horizontal railings.

Stacked stone.

Brick and iron give a traditional feel.

Gates and Ar

Casual, but elegant.

In addition to many varied fence styles, there are countless unique gates. Quite often, it is a gate to the outdoor rooms or small side yards that are the real visual jewels. They can be an enchanting and welcoming accent. Arbors crown a few of these gates. The distance between the gate and the front door oftentimes is so small that the two function together as a single design element.

Garden jewel.

A gate and a front door are paired at the entry.

Clean lines and stylish.

A gate as individual as the home.

An entry for a hacienda.

Celebrating sea life.

Often the gate reflects the home's architecture.

This gate reflects the craftsman styled front door.

Blue accents.

An arbor announces the entry.

Patina adds charm.

Both gate and garden wall are integral to the house.

A gate featuring the home's address.

Adding details make the fence and arbor unique.

A gate between properties.

Roses decorate an arbor.

An excellent example of Spanish Colonial Architecture.

Bougainvillea accents the gated courtyard.

The popularity of Spanish Colonial Revival architecture in Southern California is reflected in many of the beach homes. This style was especially popular in the coastal communities during the 1920s. A house constructed around an interior courtyard is just one of the structural elements for this style where ornate gates often function as front doors. A large or full-size gate may be less inviting, but is certainly practical and can be just as attractive. These gates and doors are as individual as the homes and the homeowners.

The home is entered through the courtyard gate.

A door as a gate.

Homes behind these gates can be quite modest.

A translucent gate transmits light.

One of the many full-sized gates that isolate homes from street traffic.

Landscape as Bo

dary

Hedges as outdoor walls.

Hedges are often used as a variation of more typical fencing. They occasionally are pruned and trimmed to provide screening and security or kept small to resemble little fences. Larger hedges have an additional benefit of serving as natural windbreaks. Not all plantings used as barriers in the beach communities are hedges in the traditional sense. Sometimes the plantings occur just close enough together to offer the psychological privacy so needed in urban living. Dense plantings are a perfect boundary at the beach – natural and effective.

Hedges make excellent fences.

Another hedge as a wall example.

Vines create an arbor.

Landscaping and fence make a pleasant combination.

Inviting portal.

Simple and modern, reeds provide additional privacy.

Flowers decorate and divide.

Flowering boundary leads to entry.

A blooming screen.

Unique Bound

A raised deck or porch can create psychological distance for more privacy.

ries

Since residential properties are very closely laid out in the Beach Cities, sometimes boundaries between houses are barely discernible. The entries of a few homes near the beach are located down allies and narrow side streets. Instead of yards, there are only planters or dirt strips inserted into concrete. With no yards, decorative fences and gates are frequently used to separate properties or guide access to side entries. Often there is only the front door, which opens onto the street. The boundary can also become just a deck that is raised above or below street level, a handrail or decorative steps.

A living space becomes the front porch when the French doors are opened.

Planters between homes provide the only greenery.

Gates leading to small spaces can be individual and precious.

Some home entries are between residences.

There is no yard, only an alley.

Simply the front door and the street.

Shells decorate the steps to the side entry of this home.

Ornament & Ba

ndary

Pots make a patio "fence."

The human need to define personal space is universal, and over time, many creative and clever techniques have emerged to delineate the small beach spaces. Some beach dwellers simply use decoration to enclose and differentiate their property. Planters, screens, sculptures and fountains are effective and attractive solutions to help demarcate space. Frequently, ornament supplements define the existing boundary.

Ceramic planters are used in combination with a stucco wall.

Pots or garden wall?

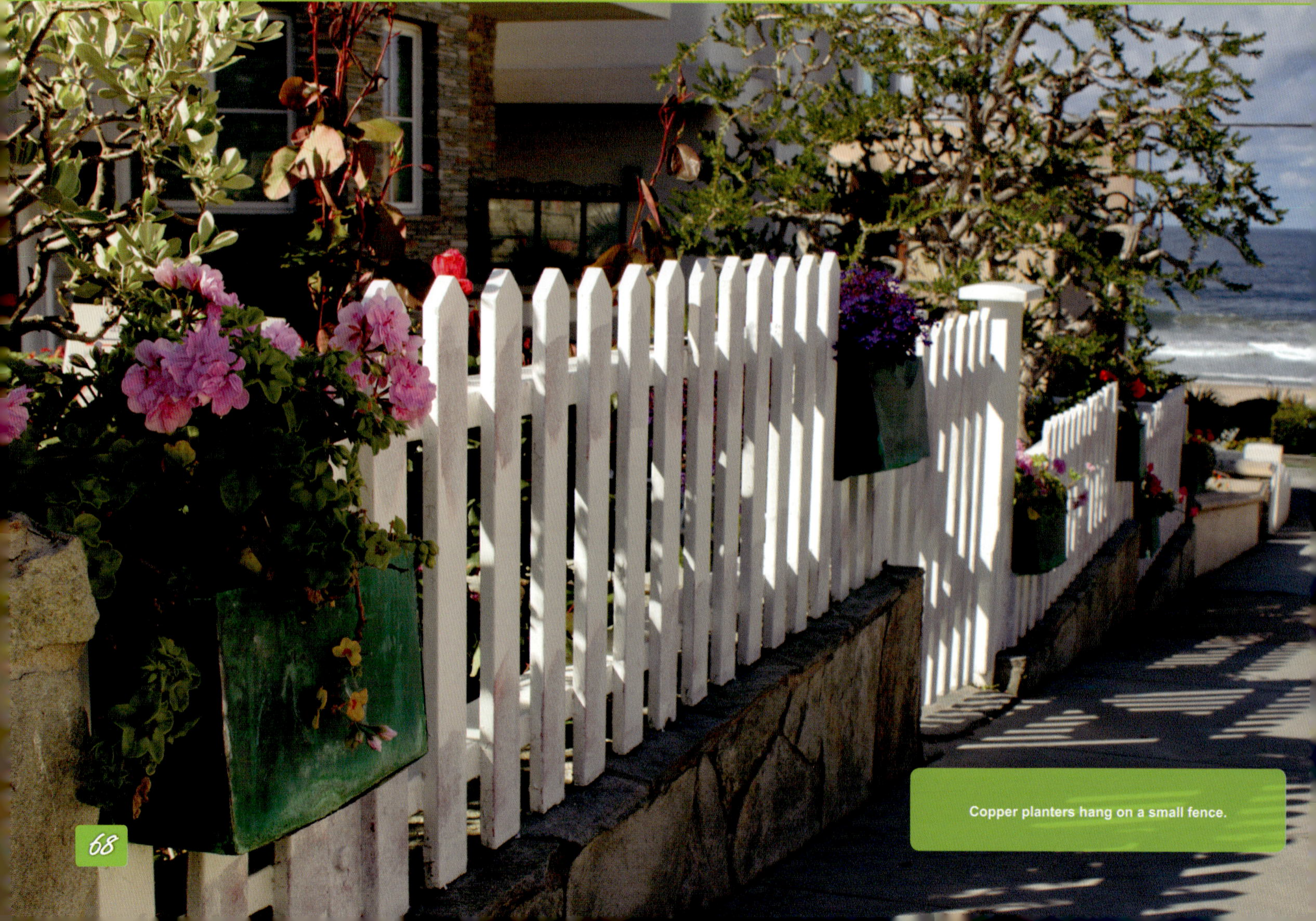

Copper planters hang on a small fence.

A hanging garden decorates a utilitarian fence.

These built-in planters make an attractive barrier.

Custom shell lanterns accent the gated walkway.

Clay pots enhance a garden wall.

A message for beach living adorns this fence.

Pots can soften a wall and increase privacy by adding height.

Having fun with your beach home.

Colorful boundaries.

Metal artist, Eric Powell, created this gate for the homeowners (ericpowell.com).

The beach at your home.

In the Beach Cities, there are echoes from an earlier time of the beach counterculture that had its origins in the Southern California surfing lifestyle. A few residences still have fun with free expression. Art or collections are used to define the boundaries. Other times, the art is within the boundary and the tiny fences let viewers admire the creative work.

Mr. Halliburton's ants surround his property.

Nautical themes – ropes and pilings create a boundary.

Mr. Halliburton's collections.

A wonderful example of this is the Halliburton Residence. Rich Halliburton, a flute maker and artist, decorates his yard like most people decorate their homes. His collection of metal sculptures, Mexican and Native American artifacts, seashells and colorful potted plants border his home and workshop.

Fences with S

Lilley Residence.

The Lilley Residence – An Inheritance:

A Grandmother Passes on a Love of Wonderful Things

As a young girl, Michelé Lilley started collecting antique keys while visiting estate sales and antique shops with her grandmother. She was fascinated with the idea of how a key could open secret doors and take her to beautiful places. There are over two hundred keys and literally thousands of seashells embedded in the walls and fences of this castle at the beach. Michelé has placed each one herself in this enchanting reflection of her love for the magic of rare and wonderful things.

Her company, Keys to My Castle, makes custom keys and allows everyone to carry a piece of their homes with them wherever they go.

Keys and shells.

Shakepark Residence.

The Shakepark Residence – A Surfing Family's Mementos

When the Shakely-Parkman family set roots in Hermosa Beach, Mr. Parkman discovered reusing old and broken surfboards was part of the funky beach spirit. Seeing surfboards as folk art, he creatively cut and hung old boards to fit on an unattractive fence by their driveway. The surfboard fence has been part of this street for a long time and a few neighbors still remember when the boards in this "art gallery" were ridden and broken by the family's son and his surfer friends. Now the fence is mostly an attraction for the kids coming down the small lane on their way home from the local high school. They stop and look to see the names, designs and shapes of the boards. The fence has been up for so long it is part of the personality of their neighborhood and beach lane.

The Haueter Residence – A Gate for Reminiscence

The Haueters, a longtime Manhattan Beach family, was planning on hosting a backyard rehearsal dinner party for their son's wedding. Because of this special family event, it was decided that a fence located near the front door needed to be replaced with something more beautiful and inviting. Chris Haueter, the groom, designed and built this unique structure to mark the occasion. Chris's father passed away shortly after the wedding and this handcrafted gate of iron and redwood is a lovely reminder of that summer evening's gathering.

Haueter Residence.

Parker Residence.

The Parker Residence – A Surfer's Gate

Bill and Laurie Parker both grew up in the Southern California beach communities. Bill built the gate to their home after his surfboard met its untimely demise one morning while he was surfing. Bill's life has always been about the ocean, so instead of throwing it away, he was able to salvage it and a few memories of fun times by installing the board as a gate to their home. Those memories are now left hanging on the side of their house. While the neighbors may comment that the gate is somewhat unusual, Bill thinks it contributes to the quirky appeal of Hermosa Beach.

The Myer Residence – An Editorial Comment for Beach Living

This fence, with its humorous comment, has been part of Manhattan Beach's surfer lore for quite some time. A few years ago, it was featured in the *Los Angeles Times* newspaper making it even more of a local landmark. Mr. Myers, who surfed long ago and is now retired, painted his comment on a whim. The message celebrates our beach location and counters what most of us consider a drudging reality – work!

Myers Residence.

The Woodcock Residence, designed and built by Michael Woodcock,

mrwdesigndevelopment.com